TRANSPORT IN MY COMMUNITY

AEROPLANES

by Cari Meister

raintree

a Capstone company — publishers for children

Aeroplanes take us all over the world. People travel for work, for holidays and to visit family and friends. Aeroplanes can carry goods, letters and parcels too!

Aeroplanes can also be
called "planes" for short.

Let's fly!

Aeroplanes are amazing flying machines.
They are huge and heavy but they can stay
in the sky for hours.

How do they work?

The pilot sits in the cockpit. The co-pilot sits next to the pilot. They control all the buttons and switches to make the aeroplane fly.

The buttons and switches are on the instrument panel. There are lots of screens too. They show how high the aeroplane is flying. The screens can also show if there are other aeroplanes nearby.

BRUMMMMM!

The pilot turns on the aeroplane's
engines. The plane roars to life.
It taxis down the runway.

The aeroplane starts to travel down the runway faster and faster. It zooms forwards very fast.

Air flows over the aeroplane's
wings. This makes the aeroplane lift
into the air.

When the aeroplane is up in the air, the wheels move up into the plane.

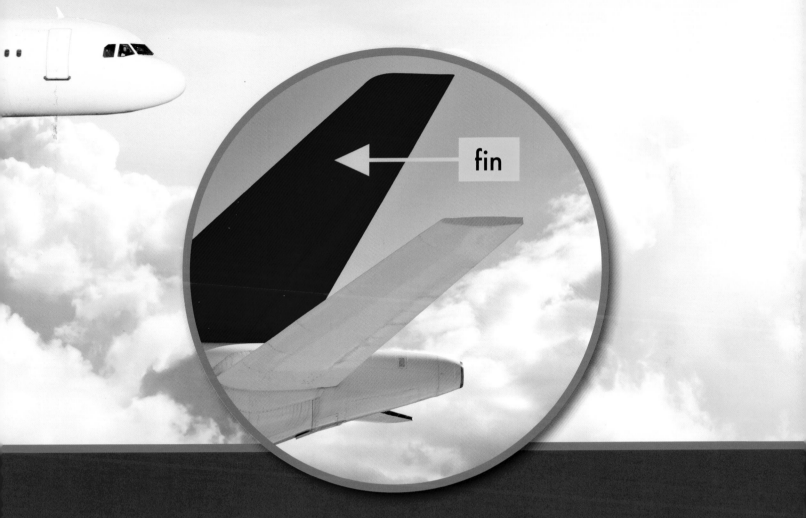

fin

Fins at the back help to keep the aeroplane level as it flies.

It's time to land.

The aeroplane slows down and starts to descend.
The pilot lowers the landing gear.
The wheels touch down on the runway.

We're here!

Aeroplanes have not always looked
like they do today.

The first powered aeroplane was light and open.
There was only room for the pilot.

Today we use aeroplanes to do lots of
different jobs.
A passenger jet carries people.

A passenger jet is like a big bus in the sky.
Some have two levels, like a double-decker bus!
They can carry more than 850 people.

A fighter jet is **FAST!**

Fighter jets are used by the armed forces. They are sometimes used in wars. They take soldiers to countries where they are needed.

Cargo planes carry goods instead of people.
Super transporters move really big things.

The *Antonov AN-225* is the world's largest type of cargo plane. It can hold and move the weight of 80 cars!

WHIRRR!

Crop dusters spread fertilizer on farm fields.
The fertilizer helps the plants grow.

Crop dusters and other small planes often have propellers. The propeller helps to lift the aeroplane into the air.

floats

SPLASH!

A seaplane does not need a runway.
It can take off and land on water.
The plane has floats instead of wheels.

Seaplanes can be used to search
for and rescue people in water.

Engineers are working to make aeroplanes safer. They are also finding ways for aeroplanes to use less fuel.

What will aeroplanes look like in the future?

Timeline

1896

The first unmanned, steam-powered aircraft flies in the United States.

1880

1903

1900

The Wright brothers fly the *Wright Flyer* for 12 seconds; it is the first powered, manned flight in history.

1927

Charles Lindberg becomes the first person to fly non-stop across the Atlantic Ocean.

1920

1930

The jet engine is invented.

1933

The *Boeing 247* is the first passenger airliner.

1947

1940

The *Bell X-1* is the first airplane to fly faster than the speed of sound.

1986

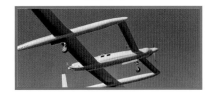

1960

The aircraft *Voyager* makes the first non-stop flight around the world.

2011

The *Transition* becomes the world's first flying car.

1980

2018

2016

The *Solar Impulse 2* becomes the first aeroplane powered by the Sun to fly around the world.

2000

Drones are being developed to inspect the outside of aeroplanes.

2020

Glossary

cockpit the area in the front of a plane where the pilot sits

co-pilot person who helps the pilot and takes over if the pilot is resting or ill

descend to move from a higher place to a lower place

engine a machine that makes power needed to move something

fertilizer a substance used to make crops grow better

goods things, usually for selling

landing gear wheels of an aeroplane

pilot driver of an aeroplane

propeller one or more blades that turn very fast; a propeller moves the plane through the air

runway long, flat piece of ground where a plane can take off or land

taxi to travel slowly along the ground

Find out more

Aeroplanes (Transport), Mari Shuh (Raintree, 2018)

How Aeroplanes Work for Kids (Baby Professor, 2017)

Planes (Usborne beginners), Fiona Patchett (Usborne, 2007)

Websites

www.sciencekids.co.nz/ sciencefacts/vehicles/airplanes
Read fast facts and trivia about aeroplanes.

www.scienceforkidsclub.com/ airplanes
Find facts about the history of aeroplanes, and how they work!

Index

Raintree is an imprint of Capstone Global Library Limited, a company incorporated in England and Wales having its registered office at 264 Banbury Road, Oxford, OX2 7DY – Registered company number: 6695582

www.raintree.co.uk
myorders@raintree.co.uk

Text © Capstone Global Library Limited 2020
The moral rights of the proprietor have been asserted.

Editor: Michelle Parkin
Designer: Rachel Tesch
Printed and bound in India

ISBN: 978 1 4747 6899 3 (hardback)   ISBN 978 1 4747 6903 7 (paperback)

British Library Cataloguing in Publication Data
A full catalogue record for this book is available from the British Library.

Acknowledgements
Alamy: Dariusz Kuzminski, 30 (bottom right), INTERFOTO, 30 (top right); Getty Images: Bettmann, 30 (left and right middle), Brooke/Stringer, 16-17, Universal History Archive, 17 (inset); iStockphoto: bkindler, 10, energy, 13 (inset), frankpeters, 8, guvendemir, 20-21, Jag_cz, 12-13, muratart, 11, Rathke, 6-7, Senohrabek, 14, serts, 9; Shutterstock: CrispyPork, 4-5, Dan Thornberg, cover (top), 1, Denis Belitsky, cover (bottom middle), frank_peters, cover (bottom right), Galyna Andrushko, cover (bottom left), Gavin Baker Photography, 24-25, Igor Karasi, 15, iurii, 29, Jag_cz, 27, oriontrail, 19, PomInOz, 26, Popsuievych, 23, Sebastian stocking, 28, Skycolors, 18, vaalaa, 22, Yasar Turanli, 2-3

Every effort has been made to contact copyright holders of material reproduced in this book. Any omissions will be rectified in subsequent printings if notice is given to the publisher.